A Collection of Poems II

Danny P. Barbare

ISBN: 978-93-6354-794-0

First Edition: 2024
Rs. 200/-

Cyberwit.net
HIG 45 Kaushambi Kunj, Kalindipuram
Allahabad - 211011 (U.P.) India
http://www.cyberwit.net
Tel: +(91) 9415091004
E-mail: info@cyberwit.net

Printed at Repro India Limited.

Contents

The Poet's Poem

Dear America
I have written this poem to you
in the ink of azaleas
on a ridge of blue
with words that buzz like
bumblebees.
This is the South, my page of
paper
this is my home, the place I
know
the rolling foothills of cursive
where you are welcome within these margins.
The pen is the tool of
the season, the cartridge of the Carolinas.

Always

Blue
sky

how
happy
am
I

without
a
sigh

not
a
bit
shy

as
if
to
me,
the
sun
always
shines.

At the Lake

Put the knee to the chest
let the boat do the pulling in
the smooth cove
go from side to side
kicking up the water
as high as you can
letting go of the rope
gliding to the dock
when hungry
for roasted corn,
homemade hushpuppies
and coleslaw,
with sunfish and bass
caught with a string , bread,
and golden claw hook.

The Canada Goose

The Canada Goose wanted to be a poem
so I took a feather and dipped
it into a bottle
of the blackest ink for eyes
and quill ,
silver gray,
nestled in my thoughts
as it began to strut as if proud
and did not seem to want to
fly away
before the bottom of the page
as it had that animated smile
as I composed and recited
coming back the next day to
find the right words like my desk
and chair beside the road
and lamp to shed a little new light
in the green blades of grass by the woods.

The Snowflake

Walking home
a snowflake
kisses me on the
cheek
fresh and cold as
winter's lips.

My boots crunch in
the February snow.

In the mirror
my skin is lipstick red.

News from the Janitor

I'm a happy janitor
dusting my troubles
  away
it's a feathery job
but not nothing to sneeze
  about
that is the very settling of
  it
to keep from growing old
  and
gray—the smut of it.

Caesar's Head

On the mountain,
I can hear the wind.
As it feathers through my hair
And blows all around,
I look before me
At the lake and land down below
And then turn and walk away
On a fair day in winter
As if I have flown
In the Heavens.

The Crow

A crow in the yard
has half to himself.
His shadow is
like a separate self
not as dark,
and leans upon blades
of grass,
until crow gives the shadow
wings.

The Sprouts

Sprouts of sunlight
Push through the black clouds.
The seedlings grow
Into trees of sunshine
That spread on the shadowed earth
Drenched with brown leaves.

The Janitor

Getting into the routine
  emptying trash
the old clock inside me
  begins to hum along
  a steady tick
as if the red hand quickens
  to the hour.

The Broom's Job

Says
the
broom

handle
and
straw

it's
my
job

to
make
shoes
happy.

The Broom and I

The broom says let's
  talk
and be happy
we don't have to be
  lonely
and the day will whistle
  and sing by.

The Apple Orchard and Store

It's autumn. At the end of the gravel
road
there is a building where they
sell apple butter, cider, chow
chow
and pepper jelly and other goods.
Some choose to pick their own
apples
in the orchard
while others buy them by the
bushel or peck full
to last them throughout winter
warm pie for Thanksgiving or
just a Golden Delicious for a snack
as snow settles in always a crisp
bite of fall.

Carl Sandburg's Pond

Yesterday, I visited
Carl Sandburg's pond.

It was empty
and overgrown with
weeds.

But with words I knew
I could
fill it with water, fish
and ducks
and bring the waterfall to life.

There, you see, it worked.

Talking About Her Flower Garden

Words
between us grew
like flowers
in good soil
from roots and
stems
like seeds they
began
pulling out the
weeds
and spreading
pine needles
and water.

Conversation

Spaces
of
a
puzzle

that
paint
a
picture
with
words

that
fit
like
conversation

happy
sound.

It's a New Day

Spring, it's a new day
the
sun sits
in a drop
of morning dew
on a blade
of grass
that tickles the
toes
and makes you
laugh
like
the child inside of you.

The Phone Call

The phone rings with joy, happy to pickup
the
hook my gleeful buttons
pushed
the line to catch
up on old times
through the cord to share
laughter through
the speaker and receiver
to set up a
meeting before the dial
tone,
in the same area code
hanging up with a smile and a calendar.

The Apple Poem

The apple wanted to be a
poem, so I told it first
of all
you have to be
sweet
whatever stem that
comes from
and with each crunch
you'll know you are
getting closer to the
core
the very seed from
which it came
and grew into a tree
producing words good
and crisp, sweeter than me.

A Ride to the Blue Ridge

Riding to the Blue Ridge Mountains
just as she loved
with rosy cheeks, and red lipstick
a white hat with a
ball on top, gloves, and a coat that all
matched. Spring and summer the
roadside stand, tomatoes and
cantaloupe. In autumn leaves and
apples as if my life with her a year
in full circle.

Remembering Hendersonville

Riding to the mountains
the weather is quite kind as
patches of clouds
make quilt work along Highway
25 as I can't even remember
how many times traveling
through Tuxedo
up to my aunt Luree's and
uncle AV's.
on a gravel road where aunt
Sallie sat
in a rocking chair on her
front porch
with round glasses and
a bible on her lap
as Highway 26 could be
seen in the distance
beyond a red Mack Tractor
in a corn field.
I remember my uncle's
Cub Cadet and their garden
that grew my aunt Luree's
delicious cream corn, I really
need to keep up with my
cousins and not be like a
crow and a scarecrow
as they are not so faraway—
where the best apples grow.

Mountain Poem

Words
on
a
piece
of
paper

are
just
the
ink

of
The
Blue
Ridge.

Apple Sauce

Take
care

and
life
will
be
sweet

like
whip
cream
on
apple
sauce.

Strawberry Hill

Strawberry in a cone
butter
pecan and
peach
in cups
delicious on our
tongues
homemade fields
and fields
nice and cold
the teeth
think awhile.—
A sweet day
three crumpled
napkins say
so, like
bellies
full of
buckets of ice cream.

Camp Old Indian

During Order of the Arrow
we could not speak
or else a notch would be
carved in the stick
around our necks
and we would be paddled.
I slept by the lake wrapped
around a tree. I slept so
soundly the frogs, crickets,
cicadas, didn't even bother
me. I overslept and a friend
had to wake me up for
breakfast. At the end of the
initiation we didn't get
paddled at all and
got awarded for our efforts.

A Blade of Grass

It's spring, a new day
the sun
sits
on a drop
of morning dew
on a blade of
grass
that tickles
your toes
and makes you laugh
like the child inside of you.

In the Wind

Poetry in the wind
add a little sun
and blue sky
and the words will
sing like a songbird
as colorful as a
bottle of ink
written in the trees
or across the page.

My Dream

Happy
go
lucky

the
sun
in
her
eyes

makes
me
dream

silver
necklace
and
butterfly.

A Blackbird

A blackbird with yellow
eyes is happy in a
yard of ripe pecans
that tatter through the
leaves into the hands
of the blades of grass.

Mountains of Trees!

Mountains
of
green

I
am
rich

hear
me
breathe

thankful
to
the
leaves
on
trees.

My Favorite Desk

I find an excuse for my wife and
I to go to the
blue ridge
so I can write a poem
as if it gives me a pen and
a piece of paper
with a good hand
at the steering wheel
to create
as my ears pop and
my world is silent with my
thoughts at my favorite
desk
as in October there is
mountains of ideas like colorful
leaves
and apples to write across
the blue line
as words are as green as
mountain laurel
and find
a home with a view like a ridge.

A Black-Eyed Pea

A black-eyed pea is already
off the plate onto the maple
table. I try to pick it up without
mashing the resolution
between my fingers. Oh how
tasty is the New Year like a
strip of bacon, like a heap of
serving spoon like a field—

Blueberry Muffins

Licking the blueberry mix
from the spoon
dripping it into the cupcake
pan, the aroma overflows
from the oven, golden brown.

Pickled Beets

Sweet
pickled
beets

stain
my
memory

like
my
tongue.

A Friend

Sharing
time
together

whatever
shape
cloud
that
maybe

silence
is
golden
as
sunshine.

The Dog

No matter how singled out you
feel
how much rain and dark
the clouds
the dog just doesn’t seem
to care
you’re his sun and sun alone.

A Poem Is

Sweeping
away

a
poem
is
in
everything

beneath
the
dirt
and
grime

a
word
that
shines.

Worldwide

Laughing
with

not
at

makes
the
world
like
one
big
backyard

with
a
house
and
red
barn.

Building Its Winter Nest

A
Carolina
Wren
flitters
about
in
the
flower
pot

still
with
red
blossoms.

It
goes
and
comes
with
its
tail
cocked
up

as
if
it
is

building
its
winter
nest.

At the End of the Mica Asphalt

Where the mica asphalt road ends
in the brush
clear water ebbs in the sandy
muddy shore. Shiny bubbles
pop. Tree roots gnarl in
the open.
The navy blue water is
white capping near and far.
Bass boats
skim with a tiny hum. The
house on the hill is
surrounded by a grassy yard.
It's a windy autumn day
as I wear my breaker ruffling
and my blue jeans seem thin.
The sun is a peaceful loneliness.
The woody
colors have their own certain quiet.

At the Boat Ramp

Putting in the cock plug. Releasing the nylon rope
and hook.
The car backs up, stops.
The two tone
Glassmaster
rolls off the trailer into
the still water. The stern
is lowered.
The key turned in the
ignition. The OMC
inboard
rumbles awake. The tanks are full. It's spring.

The Gazebo Alone

Winter quiet. Gazebo.
Two rusty soda machines.
Gray picnic tables and
benches. The wind passing
through. I think it is a
rainy day. Cold. Words like
nails in the boards,
lattice work like poetry.
I have it all to myself the
smell of woods. Poems like
shelter keeping me dry.
The love of nature, here
when I was in my alone.

Thunderstorm

Outside
the
bedroom
window

thunder
rain

a
pillow
a
comforter

strange.

Chicken Coops

Pen wire
empty blue
bottles
of medicine
rotten wood
a rabbit
trap old and
rusty closed
at the end of
a chain
not a worry
invincible.

The Mop Dances

With a twist of the hips
and a shuffle
of the feet
the mop says hang onto
my handle and we shall
shine on the ballroom
floor in the
spotlight
good and sweet and clean.

At the Cemetery

Storm or wind, sister tending
to the family
flowers.
Plastic, cloth, or fresh
they never seem to wither
or fade, blow
away, as if it was just yesterday.

Pots and Pans

How funny it seems
how happy I am
when I'm doing my chores
after sitting at a computer all day
hear the rattle of the pots and pans
like the music of a tambourine
oh how warm the water is.

The Window

To
see
good
in
everyone

is
a
reflection
on
you

says
the
janitor
with
a
rag
and
a
bottle
of
spray.

The Janitors Sweep

It's
so
you
know
which
broom
is
which

good
hard
work

dirt
and
grit.

Visit to the Mountains

Homeward bound
passing
the
mountain
laurel
and
Rhododendron
after seeing
a heaven
of tulips
and reaching
out
and touching the sky.

Sunshine

She
passes
by
with
a
smile
in
her
eyes

as
if
today
and
tomorrow

will
be
filled
with
sunshine.

Body Surfing

Body surfing, waiting for
the right swell
the right timing
it picks my feet up
I swim into the white
crest
feeling the power of the
water
crashing around me
it takes me to the beach
and
it puts me upon my feet.

The Candle

Memories
of
dad
are
still
aglow

warm
like
the
tears
of
a
candle

that
drip
into
the
candle
holder

till
the
candle
no
longer
melts

but
the
tears
are
still
warm.

The Greenness

Feeling
the
first
sun

is
the
beginning
of
the
greenness
in
the
grass
and
trees

the
unfurling
of
the
new

like
a
dream
that
has
just
taken
root.

The Jack-O-Lantern

Lighting the candle in the
jack-o-lantern
at sunset
it grows brighter
in the dark
or rather comes
alive
as if it has a mind
of its own
spooky and quiet
which
ever way
the wind flickers
till all the goblins are gone.

The Sunset's Wisdom

One
day
older

and
that
is
beautiful

as
the
sunlight
has
shed
light

orange,
pink,
and
golden.

A Slice of Pumpkin Pie

Mellow
and
sweet
with
a
soft
crust

I'm
a
slice
of
pumpkin
pie

all
the
way
down
to
the
last
crumb.

Autumn Wood

In the wood there is a glow, words
like orange
yellow, red
and gold
inspiration
in the wind with
wafting ease—
spiraling
down upon
the page as long as there are trees.

The Bluebird Sky

Imagine
a
bluebird

so
small
so
big

spreads
its
blue
wings,
orange
breasted
and
flitters
away
in
slow
motion

a
pretty
little
downy
thing

as
if
to
follow
the
sun.

My Feet

Winter
white

feeling
ankle
deep

twitching
my
toes
like
sticks.

The Cloud

Peace is like a cloud surrounded
by
golden sunshine
that billows
with happiness in the
sky
and wants nothing
else
but to be where it is perfectly still.

Seeking a Job

Into
the
light

is
where
I'm
headed

filled
with
possibility

with
the
sun
on
my
brow

and
a
good
set
of
hands.

The Christmas Angel

It's that time of year
again
when the acrylic angel
from Cracker Barrel
is taken from the shelf
in the cool back room
and put
on the TV stand in the
den and
filled with a set of
triple A batteries
as it lights up the dark
room with a switch—
her colors so spiritual.

The Church Ornament

On the mantle is a church
Christmas
ornament filled
with stirring water
and glitter
powered by
three double a
batteries and
brightly
lit. It makes me
feel like such a
wonderful
Southern wintery scene.

She

She is on her way
home, as
the fire
glows warm
and the acrylic
angel sparkles
as the phone
wants to stay
connected
and listen
till the lines meet.

The Pontoon Boat

The pontoon boat with blue and white
vinyl seats skims even on a windy
day
across the
the evening lake with its Evinrude
45 into the big water smooth as a
drink
Surrounded by a party of friends
and relatives as the sun is brilliant orange.

The Possum

Can’t sleep, get out of bed late
one night, the motion
spotlight
is on. I look out the kitchen
window and a possum is digging
in the grass where vegetable oil
was poured. I tap on the window
once, it looks, tap on it twice
and it
looks again, I finally open
the window and it
takes off running around the house.

The Leaves

Like
the
leaf
of
autumn

we
make
light
of
each
other

care
is
transparent

special
as
the
sun.

The Oil Lamp on the Table

Sitting at the table
forgetting time
looking into the
oil lamp at the flame slowly
peacefully dancing
teaching one the
slow dance of life.

Three Crows

Three
crows

we
are
all
together

what
little
of
a
mystery

I'm
one
of
two.

Mayonnaise and Chopped Apples

With a bowl and fork
life is
creamy and sweet
to me—
upon the tongue
strangely delicious
says the poet—like a poem.

The Broom Always Learning

Says
the
broom
I'm
always a
student in my
own poetic
way
when I'm
sweeping down
the steps
I'm really sweeping
up
thanks to
poetry
straw for straw
word for word
as I learn by
the
wooden handle
of things
good and
clean.

The Broom's Clue

Says the broom
this is the clue
I build others up
as that is a
reflection on me
straw for straw
I sweep with rather
than at
it's all in the timing
handle to handle
that's just plain
simple manners
and kindness.

Direction

We are father and son
standing on the porch of the
house.
Out of the millions,
he points out the North Star
using a method.
In my youth,
he was my universe.
Now, I must find direction
by the North Star
using the method he taught me
to get out of a dark wood.

Dethroned

The blue jay
was king.

Now the cat
happily purrs.

Sweet on Each Other

Honey
and
peanut
butter

are
sweet
on
each
other

like
Romeo
and
Juliet
sitting
on
a
spoon.

Classic Poems

Words fall like leaves.
Only evergreens become classics.
They're green under the snow of critics
That soon melts away.

Then, there stands the pine;
Its taste strong as always.
The sun shining on words in motion.
There is never a windless day.

The Mountains

The mountains wanted me to
write
a poem.
So I took the sky in my
hand
and wrote across the ridges
in colorful ink
because it was autumn
and the words were so
cool
the paper smelled like apples.

www.ingramcontent.com/pod-product-compliance
Ingram Content Group UK Ltd.
Pitfield, Milton Keynes, MK11 3LW, UK
UKHW041315190726
13845UKWH00025B/286

9 789363 547940